DOLLY:

THE 1ST CLONED SHEEP

Written by Joeming Dunn • Illustrated by Brian Denham

FAMOUS FIRSTS: ANIMALS MAKING HISTORY

Making
1996
History

magic
wagon

visit us at www.abdopublishing.com

Published by Magic Wagon, a division of the ABDO Publishing Group, 8000 West 78th Street, Edina, Minnesota 55439. Copyright © 2012 by Abdo Consulting Group, Inc. International copyrights reserved in all countries. All rights reserved. No part of this book may be reproduced in any form without written permission from the publisher.

Graphic Planet™ is a trademark and logo of Magic Wagon.

Printed in the United States of America, North Mankato, Minnesota.
052011
092011
This book contains at least 10% recycled materials.

Written by Joeming Dunn
Illustrated by Brian Denham
Colored by Rod Espinosa
Lettered by Doug Dlin
Edited by Stephanie Hedlund and Rochelle Baltzer
Interior layout and design by Antarctic Press
Cover art by Brian Denham
Cover design by Neil Klinepier

Library of Congress Cataloging-in-Publication Data

Dunn, Joeming W.
  Dolly : the 1st cloned sheep / written by Joeming Dunn ; illustrated by Rod Espinosa.
     p. cm. -- (Famous firsts. Animals making history)
  Includes index.
  ISBN 978-1-61641-640-9
  1. Dolly (sheep)--Juvenile literature. 2. Cloning--History--Juvenile literature. 3. Transgenic animals--Juvenile literature. 4. Famous animals--Juvenile literature. I. Espinosa, Rod, ill. II. Title.
  QH442.2D86 2012
  636.3'0821--dc22
                              2011011363

TABLE OF CONTENTS

What Is Cloning?. 5
Types of Cloning 10
The Story of Dolly. 15
Birth and Life 20
Death and Controversy 24
Dolly Facts 30
Web Sites 30
Glossary 31
Index 32

NOW, I'M NOT TALKING ABOUT A COPY FROM A PHOTOCOPY MACHINE OR A SCANNER.

I'M TALKING ABOUT CREATING AN *EXACT GENETIC COPY.*

To create life in most mammals, a male and a female each contribute genetic material.

The female produces the egg, or oocyte. It holds the genetic material from the mother.

The male produces sperm. It has the genetic material from the father.

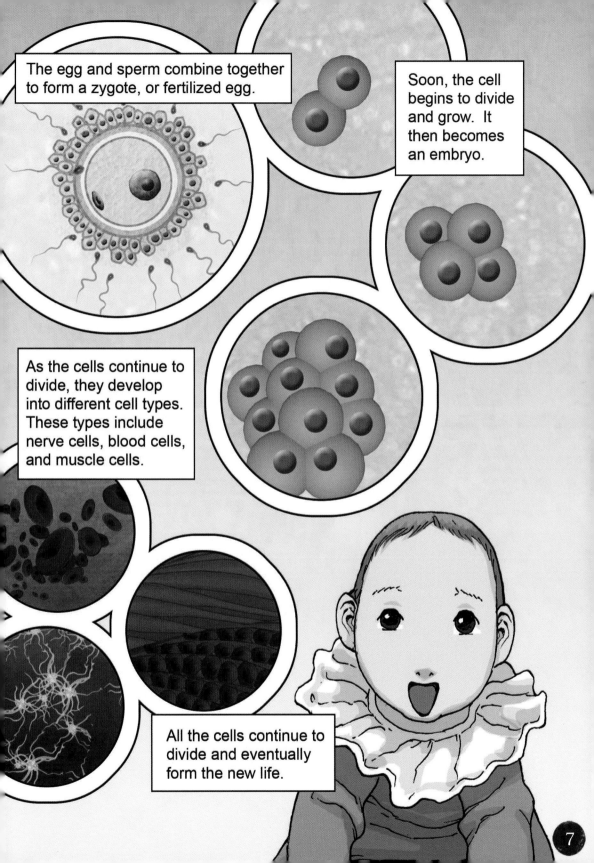

The egg and sperm combine together to form a zygote, or fertilized egg.

Soon, the cell begins to divide and grow. It then becomes an embryo.

As the cells continue to divide, they develop into different cell types. These types include nerve cells, blood cells, and muscle cells.

All the cells continue to divide and eventually form the new life.

NOW, HOW THE CELLS DECIDE WHAT TYPE OF CELLS THEY'LL BE IS A BIT COMPLICATED.

A cell has many structures in it. The part we'll be talking about is the nucleus.

Flagellum

Basal body

Smooth endoplasmic reticulum

Nucleolus

Nucleus

Chromatin

Rough endoplastic reticulum

Centriole

Vacuole

Nuclear envelope

Lysosome

Microtubules

Golgi apparatus

Ribosomes

Microvilli

Secretion being released from cell by exocytosis

Cytosol

Mitochondrio

Microfilamen

Peroxisome

Plasma membrane

The nucleus contains deoxyribonucleic acid, also known as DNA.

DNA holds all the genetic information used for the development and the functioning of all living things.

DNA is made of four units called nucleotides. The nucleotides are thymine, adenine, guanine, and cytosine. They combine in a long double spiral, or double helix, of different pairs to form the entire DNA chain.

Thymine
Adenine
Guanine
Cytosine

DNA has a lot of information. It tells the organism to build certain cells and to how to use them properly. DNA is organized in the nucleus into structures called chromosomes. Some chromosomes in the human body are *millions* of nucleotide pairs long!

The information in DNA from the mother and father helps determine personal traits. These include height, eye color, skin color, and hair color.

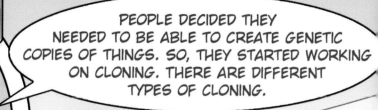

PEOPLE DECIDED THEY NEEDED TO BE ABLE TO CREATE GENETIC COPIES OF THINGS. SO, THEY STARTED WORKING ON CLONING. THERE ARE DIFFERENT TYPES OF CLONING.

One type of cloning is called gene cloning, or DNA cloning.

DNA cloning is when scientists want to reproduce just a part of a long strand of DNA. In this case, the DNA part is injected into a bacteria or virus, which can then reproduce that strand of DNA many times.

This type of cloning can help produce many types of medication, including insulin for diabetes.

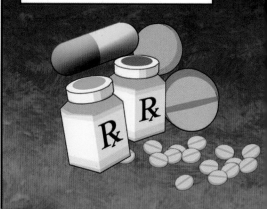

Another type of cloning is embryo cloning.

This type of cloning is used to create copies of stem cells. Scientists use these cells for research.

Stem cells are the beginning building blocks of the body. They can develop into almost any type of cell, tissue, or organ in the body.

Many scientists claim stem cells could be used to help cure diseases including Alzheimer's disease. They could also be used to replace damaged organs.

THE LAST TYPE OF CLONING IS REPRODUCTIVE CLONING. THAT'S HOW I WAS CLONED!

Remember that in a normal cycle, the egg joined with sperm to create a zygote. Then the zygote divided and developed until it became new life.

WITH ME, THE PROCESS WAS DIFFERENT.

The first step of reproductive cloning is to get an egg.

Using a microscope and a fine needle, scientists carefully remove the egg's nucleus.

With the nucleus removed, there is no genetic material in the egg.

Another needle holds a nucleus with the genetic material they want to copy. They place that DNA into the empty egg.

The egg with its new nucleus of genetic material is now ready.

The new cell is then cared for to help start division.

When the new cell starts dividing, it is implanted into its "mother." There it will grow to term.

This type of cloning was first successfully used in frogs and fish. The first frog was cloned in 1958 at Oxford University in England.

THE PROCESS USED FOR FROGS DIDN'T WORK FOR OTHER ANIMALS. MOST ATTEMPTS TO CLONE MICE OR CATTLE USED EMBRYOS. ATTEMPTS TO USE FULL-GROWN CELLS FAILED...UNTIL ME!

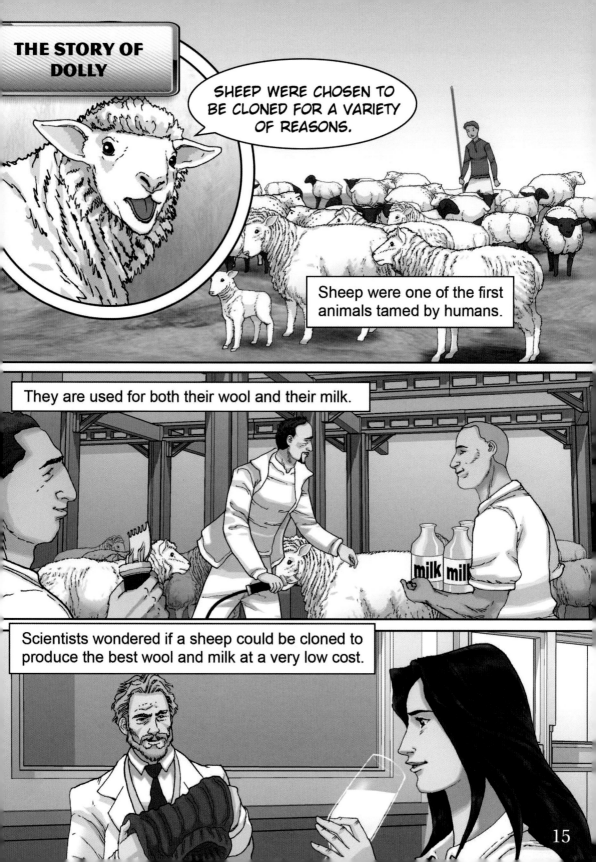

THE STORY OF DOLLY

SHEEP WERE CHOSEN TO BE CLONED FOR A VARIETY OF REASONS.

Sheep were one of the first animals tamed by humans.

They are used for both their wool and their milk.

Scientists wondered if a sheep could be cloned to produce the best wool and milk at a very low cost.

15

Some cells develop very quickly. Even in adults, some cells continue to cycle very fast, like those in skin or hair.

Other cells, such as nerve cells, do not cycle very fast.

Originally, scientists thought a nucleus transfer should occur in fast-dividing cells. They thought this would help the embryo grow fast.

But Campbell and Wilmut decided to try replacing a nucleus that was not developing at all.

They chose to clone a six-year-old, female, Finn Dorset domesticated sheep.

They removed cells from the sheep's mammary gland.

An egg donor was chosen. She was a Scottish Blackface sheep.

The cells of each were then isolated.

To start the reproductive cloning, the nucleus was removed from each of the Blackface's eggs.

Then the nucleus of the Finn Dorset's mammary cell was removed.

The mammary cell nucleus was then inserted into one of the eggs.

After the nucleus was placed, the new cell was shocked with an electrical current. This helped start cell division.

19

The cell began to divide. When it reached blastocyst stage, it was ready to be placed in the mother.

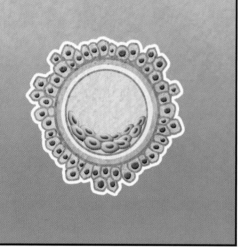

Other Scottish Blackface sheep were chosen to carry the developing eggs.

The process was quite difficult. Campbell and Wilmut tried 277 cell fusions, but only 29 continued to grow after the electric shock.

The embryos were then divided and implanted into 13 different Scottish Blackface sheep.

The mothers were watched very carefully.

As time went on, most of the pregnancies failed.

Only one pregnancy went to full term. On July 5, 1996, I was born! I weighed about 15 pounds (7 kg).

I was the first clone that was produced from an adult mammal. So I basically had three parents.

I was born healthy and was suckling within minutes of birth.

I was treated especially well at the Roslin Institute. I never left the institute, but they took great care of me.

I always slept inside, mostly so I would not be stolen or get lost.

Dolly

When I got older, I was mated with a Welsh Mountain Ram.

I soon had children of my own. In April 1998, I gave birth to my first lamb, named Bonnie.

In 1999, I had twin lambs named Sally and Rosie. And in fall 2001, I had triplets named Lucy, Darcy, and Cotton.

When I was five years old, I started to develop arthritis, a joint disease. Medication seemed to help for a time.

In February 2003, I started to have difficulty breathing. I had a lung disease.

My arthritis also seemed to be getting worse.

After the scientists talked about it a lot, they decided I shouldn't have to suffer with both the lung disease and arthritis. So they decided to put me down.

Dolly

I was put to sleep on February 14, 2003. I was six years old.

DICKINSON AREA
PUBLIC LIBRARY

There was a lot of debate right after my death.

A Finn Dorset sheep normally lives for 11 to 12 years, but I only lived for six years.

Many believed that my arthritis and lung disease showed that I'd aged early. Roslin scientists disagreed, saying that many indoor sheep develop the same lung disease.

It was further claimed that because my cells multiplied while I was alive, my DNA was slowly beginning to come apart and shorten. This usually happens in old age, and it happened in me.

Some people suspect that my Finn Dorset mother died at 6 years, so I was destined to die at the same age.

Even with my success, cloning remains controversial.

Cloning has many political, religious, and medical opponents.

Even though scientists know the cloning process, it is not perfected. Many failures have occurred since my case.

There have been some successes, including the cloning of cows, mules, cats, and piglets. A Black Angus cow was cloned at Texas A&M University in 2000. It had a unique immune system that resisted many diseases.

It is believed that certain types of cloning would benefit humankind.

Cloning may also help keep endangered species alive or even bring back animals that have died out.

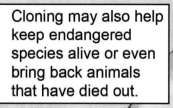

EVEN THOUGH I ONLY LIVED SIX YEARS, I CAPTURED THE IMAGINATION OF SCIENTISTS THROUGHOUT THE WORLD.

DOLLY FACTS

Name: Dolly
Age: Lived to be six years old
Weight: 15 pounds (7 kg) at birth
Breed: Finn Dorset sheep

Making 1996 History

Birth date: July 5, 1996
Birth site: Roslin Institue, University of Edinburgh, Scotland

Result: Dolly the sheep was created at the Roslin Institute as part of research into producing medicines in the milk of farm animals. The development of cloning technology has led to new ways to produce medicines. It is improving our understanding of development and genetics.

WEB SITES

To learn more about Dolly, visit ABDO Group online at **www.abdopublishing.com**. Web sites about Dolly are featured on our Book Links page. These links are routinely monitored and updated to provide the most current information available.

GLOSSARY

blastocyst stage – the stage of cell development when the cells have divided to form a small ball.

controversial – of or relating to a discussion marked by strongly different views.

domesticated – adapted to life with humans.

embryo – an organism in the early stages of development.

fusion – the combining of two different nuclei to form a cell.

genetic – of or relating to a branch of biology that deals with inherited features.

immune system – the body system that protects the body from foreign cells, tissues, and diseases.

implant – to insert a living tissue.

isolated – separated from others.

mammary gland – the gland that produces milk, which female mammals feed their young.

nucleus – the cell organ that is needed for cell functions.

organism – a living being.

reproductive cloning – producting a genetic duplicate of a living organism.

stem cells – the beginning building blocks of the body.

unique – being the only one of its kind.

INDEX

B
birth 21, 23
blastocyst stage 20

C
Campbell, Keith
   16, 17, 20
chromosomes 9

D
death 25, 26
diseases 11
DNA 8, 9, 10, 13,
   26
DNA cloning 10

E
egg 6, 7, 12, 13,
   18, 19, 20
embryo 7, 14, 17,
   20
embryo cloning
   11

G
genetic material 5,
   6, 8, 13

H
heath 23, 24, 25,
   26

L
lambs 24

N
nucleotides 9
nucleus 8, 9, 13,
   17, 19

O
Oxford University
   14

R
reproductive
   cloning 12, 13,
   14, 18, 19

Roslin Institute
   16, 23, 26

S
sperm 6, 7, 12
stem cells 11
T
Texas A&M
   University 28

W
Wilmut, Ian 16,
   17, 20

Z
zygote 7, 12